Dedication

This book is dedicated to anyone without a voice and to those who spoke up on our behalf so we could enjoy the lives we have. **This book is the Shit!**

Context is everything. Right is no longer right and wrong is no longer wrong when context is applied. When speaking up you must understand that you will offend people who fail to put things into context. Stubbornness to accept context due to delivery of message will be the cause some people to never advance in life due to lack of understanding. As a people we must learn to listen through words and hear the "message". We also must learn to speak in a way to capture as many people as possible without losing our dignity and sacrificing our soul. This is a very fine line to achieve. This book is the shit and you will enjoy every bit of it. Listen with both ears, read with ALL eyes open, and respond with an open heart.

Table of Contents

Introduction (Say It Loud) SHIT!

Let's get it out of the way. What, you may ask. The elephant in the room. The word shit. Let's get it out of our systems. Let's be comfortable with being uncomfortable before we start talking about effective ways to speak up. Say it three times. SHIT! SHIT! SHIT! Now go to someone and say it out loud three times. SHIT! SHIT! SHIT!. Now say, "I am the shit. This shit does not phase me. I need to take a...." Well, let's stop there.

Now, let's take some time to look at the power of words and the context of how they are used. If you grew up like me, you know that any four-letter words said as a kid could land you on a significant punishment. The punishment was always determined by not only which four-letter word you used but the context in which it was used. If someone said "shit" after stubbing their toe and their parent found out about it, the punishment may not be as severe as someone saying "You ain't shit" to their sibling. Society has changed, and so has the context of words. There is a time to say some words, and other times we must refrain from them because of the audience we are trying to reach. Shit talking is about speaking up and being heard.

Let's not confuse talking shit with talking bullshit. We will dive a little deeper into what it means when someone is talking bullshit.

It was 4th down and one yard to go. The sun was shining, and the smell of the fresh-cut grass entered my nostrils with each inhale I took. My mouthpiece was full of saliva and slowly dripping out of my mouth onto my hand as I stood in a three-point stance. I had one job and one job only to complete for our season to continue. My assignment was to block the middle linebacker. As the quarterback reached into his mouth and licked his fingers, he turned around and looked at me and the running back before he squatted into position and had the ball snapped. Right before he made the call, I had flashbacks of the running back, "Huff, I need you to do your job," before we approached the line.

Then, I heard another person say, "Do your fucking job!" Then the coaches yelled at all of us to do our jobs.

The defense shouted some obscenities at us to deter us from our mission. They shouted, "You suck!" "I am going to smash you!" "Y'all should give up!" "Bring that shit!" "Let's fuck them up!" The shit-talking was at an all-time high. At this point, we had a decision to make about what we heard.

The Quarter Back yelled, "Green 19! Green 19! Set! Hut!" The ball entered his hands. He dropped back two steps and handed the ball to the running back.

Knowing I was the key to the play, I ran full speed ahead into the biggest shit- talker on the team, the middle linebacker. One would think that he was all out of words, considering the game was all over and the ball was in play. Nope.

As I approached him with full speed, he shouted, "I'm, gonna FUCK you up number four!"

Lucky me, I was number four. I looked him in his eyes and shouted a war cry, like the sound the army made in the movie *300*. He hesitated because he hadn't heard that sound from me before. That was a big mistake on his end because I was in full steam ahead and ready to eat his lunch. BOOOOOOOOM! I pancake blocked him. The running back ran past me and into the end zone untouched. As I lay on top of him, I shouted, "Talk that shit now"!

Welcome to my world. I will share how you can effectively talk shit or speak up appropriately. You will learn different methods of speaking up, when is a good time to speak up, and the power of not speaking up at all. Most importantly, you will learn how to validate your shit-talking.

Defining Talking Shit

Talking shit often has a bad rap because the two words just don't seem to go together. Seriously, think about it. Shit should not come from one's mouth. As a health care professional, I understand that if a person has shit coming out of their mouth, they are in serious trouble. They may have a lower gastrointestinal blockage. However, today, talking shit happens often. Although talking shit is not recommended from a medical standpoint, it is recommended when you do it the right way.

Definition: Talking Shit – Speaking up, sharing facts, explaining your rationale for decision making.

Defining talking shit is essential, so you understand the context of the following readings. Now that the title got you to purchase the book, allow the book to teach you how to effectively speak up so that you are heard when it counts.

Shit Happens...Deal with It

Shhhhhh, can you hear that? Shhhhhhhhhh, seriously, stop talking and listen closely. Can you hear that? Shhhhhhhhhhh, but seriously, can you hear that?

At this point, you are probably asking yourself what I am talking about.

Hold up. Can you hear it now? The thoughts are racing in your head as you read the previous lines. The ideas you had regarding what you should be hearing. The thoughts that made you possibly wonder if this was an audiobook with no audio—the thoughts you had regarding what in the world you should be hearing.

Yes, that's what you should've heard. Still, you never heard what you thought because you were focused on something else. Talking shit is about first capturing and acknowledging your thoughts, dealing with your thoughts, deciding your thoughts, and finally, speaking up. The process of speaking up starts with the experiences you have in your life and your willingness to speak up. One hundred percent of the shots you do not take will equate to 100% missed shots. 100% of the time you spend holding in your words for a good cause will be 100% of the opportunities you fail to make better. The power of speaking up can save lives, change lives, and empower you to become the best version of yourself.

Events happen at a rapid pace. Some experiences we plan; others randomly come to us. Some experiences we love and others we hate to relive. The ones we love we replay over and over in our head like a song on repeat because of the feeling it gives us. Happiness, joy, satisfaction, and a sense of accomplishment are a few of those feelings.

As for the negative experiences, we often try to forget them as soon as possible because of our feelings when we replay that tragic moment. The feelings of pain, defeat, loneliness, and failure plague our minds and capture our tongues, sending us into a depressed state of mind.

Regardless of the experience, one must first be able to capture their thoughts. Capturing thoughts can often feel like casting a line in a body of water where you know there are fish, but nothing is biting your line. The ideas are there, but your mind is so busy that capturing a thought almost seems impossible. Call a time out on the play. Time outs are used in sports to regroup and come up with a plan. Time outs are critical in the medical field. They are called before a surgeon cuts a patient. The surgeon wants to make sure they perform surgery on the correct patient and the right body part.

Verification of the patient's identity is imperative. The surgeon must surround themselves with a competent team that speaks up when they feel or see something that is not safe. This is the same for you when capturing your thoughts. Call a time out. Look around you to see if you have a competent team of people who support you and want you to succeed. If they are incompetent or do not want to see you succeed, get rid of them immediately. They will negatively impact your ability to speak up.

Refer to other Wave Makers book titles to learn how to deal with people you need to cut loose.

The characteristics of the people surrounding you should include honor, integrity, loyalty, and commitment. These characteristics are essential to the growth you will gain when they support you.

How do you capture your thoughts? Call a time out and find a quiet place. It could be your car, the bathroom, an open field, the beach, or even a closet in your home. When you are situated, capture your thoughts on paper or your phone or tablet. I call this process brain dumping. Brain dumping is an effective way to determine what's essential or not by organizing your thoughts and competing priorities. Take a deep breath and write it out. Don't write it out with a plan to conquer it all. Write it out to know you will organize it based on priority. I'll give it a live shot as I write this book so you can see what I mean. Below is a real-time brain dump.

- How long will it take to write this book?

- Wave Makers book sales are up.

- I had the talk with my kids about being black in America.

- George Floyd was killed. What am I going to do about it?

- My wife is cool.

- My dogs make me happy.

- Social distancing during COVID is tearing the economy up.

- I'm hungry.

You have just read a real brain dump. I let it go. I was authentic and transparent. I told the truth and did not hide any thoughts from my thoughts. There they are, and I must deal with them. This is how you capture your thoughts. After you've completed this, walk away and let it sit. Don't do anything with it right away. Allow your mind to rest, knowing that you know what you have going on. Sometimes we have so much in our mind that we "feel" we have 100 things to do when, in fact, we may only have ten things to do.

Now that you have taken time away from your brain dump session return to deal with the thoughts. Dealing with your thoughts is the next thing you must do. To deal with your thoughts, you must prioritize them. This process is fundamental. If you are going to speak up or talk shit, you must ensure you are timely in your delivery, so your words have all the power behind them you need them to have. Below are my thoughts prioritized after writing them down.

- I am hungry.

- I had the talk with my kids about being black in America.

- My wife is cool.

- George Floyd was killed.

- Social distancing is tearing up the economy.

- My dogs make me happy.

- Wave Makers book sales are up.

- How long will it take for me to write this book?

The time it takes to brain dump will take twice as much time to prioritize and organize your list once you have the thoughts on a paper. Now that you have prioritized the items, step away and give your mind some time to relax. You can now somewhat relax because you're organized. The art of talking shit must be mastered in the mind before words exit your mouth, before your voice fills the air, and before anyone hears what you have to say or see what you do.

Now, it's time to return and act on the list of priorities. Here's what I did.

- **I am hungry.** I ordered food that made me happy—breakfast food, of course.

- **I had the talk with my kids about being black in America.** I purchased two books by Maya Angelou to gift my kids, <u>A Letter to My Daughter</u> and <u>I Know Why the Caged Bird Sings</u>. I bought these books because I realized they needed to understand the power of poetry and to articulate their feelings.

- **My wife is cool.** I smacked her on her butt. She likes that. It's like being in high school and doing something and not getting caught. Well, now it's the kids who act like we are in trouble if we show affection.

- **George Floyd was killed.** I'll tell my story in a painting.

- **Social distancing is tearing up the economy.** Develop more patience. I am considering multiple streams of revenue.

- **My dogs make me happy.** Take a photo with my dog. Post it on social media to share my happiness.

- **Wave Makers book sales are up.** Schedule time to create a flyer for incarcerated people to purchase the book and get the motivation needed to make waves.

- **How long will it take for me to write this book?** It will be done when it's done.

Whew. What a process! Now, you give it a try.

Capturing Thoughts Exercise

Search for a quiet place for your brain dump. Where is

your quiet place?

_____

_____

_____

_____

_____

_____

_____

_____

_____

_____

Brain Dump (Write down your thoughts as they come to your mind)

_____

_____

_____

_____

_____

_____

_____

_____

_____

_____

_____

Prioritize the previous list based on importance.

_____

_____

_____

_____

_____

_____

_____

_____

_____

_____

_____

For each item you wrote down, take some time to figure out how you will address each issue.

Issue 1:

_____

_____

_____

Issue 2:

_____

_____

_____

Issue 3:

_____

_____

_____

Issue 4:

_____

_____

_____

What will you do to hold yourself accountable to your plan?

_____

_____

_____

_____

_____

_____

_____

Talking Bullshit - There Is a Difference

The year was 1994, and my friends and I were on our way to school. Everyone morning, we would meet up in the projects at my friend's house, raid his snack cabinet, and ask his mother for quarters so we could go to the corner store and buy more snacks. This day was like any other day as we walked to school and discussed the things important to middle school students like games, girls, sports, and how to rap. There was always a friendly competition between us to see who was the first to have something. We talked about clothes, sneakers, and video games and debated which of us would acquire the items first.

One of my friends blurted out, "Guess what, y'all? I have Madden Football Game 1996!" We all slowed down our walk and looked at him in awe. The year was 1994, and he had a game that wasn't supposed to be available until two years later. The crowd immediately started to yell at him about how he was a liar. He stood on his word and began to convince the majority by explaining how the game looked and the new features. After 20 minutes of discussing the new game, we were all believers. My friend was a great bullshitter. He could bullshit his way through a conversation and convince people that he had something that never existed. This is my first memory of running into someone who was talking bullshit.

Bullshit can be defined as making stupid, false, or foolish comments. When someone tells false accusations or untrue stories, you may feel irritated, depending on the topic of their bullshit. My friend's goal was achieved. He had persuaded everyone that he had a game from the future. Our friendship took a turn for the worse when everyone realized he was a liar. Once everyone realized he was a liar, they discounted everything he said from that point forward. This was unfortunate because one lie has turned our view of him into a lifetime liar. Recovering from talking bullshit will take many conversations and proof of truth. If you've been the person who spoke bullshit, here is how you can attempt to make things right.

Take ownership over whatever it is that you said. You could have lied about how much money you have or where you went to school. It doesn't matter what the lie was. What matters is that you tell the truth about whatever bullshit you were sharing. This may be tough for those who play the victim role. Bear with them as they attempt to hold themselves accountable. Taking ownership over your words allows the healing process to start, not only for those you affected but also within yourself. The goal is to develop the self-confidence to speak the truth, even if insecurity encourages you to do otherwise.

Next, apologize to those you deceived. Apologies go farther than many people think when rebuilding relationships. I know. I know. I can almost hear you yelling, "What if they lie all the time and apologize all the time?" I am not referring to the habitual liar-apologizer. The definition of insanity is doing the same thing over and over and expecting different results. If someone is a habitual liar and you forgive them time and time again, you are part of the problem. Forgive, but don't accept the apology. Yes, it is possible to forgive people and not to take their apologies. Forgiveness frees you from taking more bullshit into your ears. By not accepting their apology, you let them know where you stand.

Now that you have apologized, ask the person what it will take to make the situation right. Ask them with the intent of exploring options ranging from changing your behavior to simple acts like taking them out to dinner. You never know what someone will ask of you when it comes to making things right. Nonetheless, be sure whatever they ask of you that is fair and reasonable.

The Bullshit Exercise

Write down a time you talked bullshit. This can be personal or professional, such as lying about your age, telling someone you found them attractive when you didn't, or telling your boss you completed an assignment when you had not even started.

_____

_____

_____

_____

_____

_____

_____

_____

_____

Write down the truth regarding the situation.

_____

_____

_____

_____

_____

_____

_____

_____

_____

_____

_____

Write down why you said that bullshit.

_____

_____

_____

_____

_____

_____

_____

_____

_____

_____

Write an apology to the person or group of people you deceived.

_____

_____

_____

_____

_____

_____

_____

_____

_____

_____

Ask the person affected how you can make the situation

right.

_____

_____

_____

_____

_____

_____

_____

_____

_____

_____

Write down what you are going to do to change this

behavior.

_____

_____

_____

_____

_____

_____

_____

_____

_____

_____

_____

Some of you may want to know what happened to my friend. We are still friends. He learned to back his shit up. He is now a successful professional who no longer plays video games and tells the truth about life lessons to help others see more clearly.

Responding to Ignorance – It's Clap Back Season

Jay-Z said what?

It was the summer of 1999 when a young up and coming rapper finally took his shot at the big-time rappers. Curtis "50 Cent" Jackson had enough of not being noticed and wanted to make sure he was recognized for his lyrical ability. The summer was hot with albums dropping from Snoop Dog, Ja Rule, Mase, Missy Elliot, RZA, GZA, Hot Boy$, Memphis Bleek, Ludacris, and Mobb Deep. How could a new artist be heard when all these incredible albums were being released? Nonetheless, 50 Cent took his shot and prepared for the backlash.

Jay-Z is a man of many words. His lyrical approach to sharing stories is equivalent to being the CNN or Fox News of the hood. Jay-Z has the rhythmic power to influence both inner cities and affluent areas around the world. He is well respected for his business portfolio. 50 Cent went on a rampage, lyrically attacking any rapper he felt could best. His style was generated from the historical ways of battle rapping, which is a form of verbally settling differences amongst peers. You may remember some of the names like Kool Mo Dee, Busy Bee Starksy, and KRS One, some of the battle rap pioneers from the '80s. 50 Cent channeled his rap ancestors with his own twist. That twist was aggressive and disrespectful. 50 Cent dissed seven well-known rappers, including Wu-Tang, Big Pun, Missy Elliot, Wyclef Jean, and Kurupt. One would think this was career suicide, but 50 Cent was hungry and willing to do whatever it took to get people's attention.

Of all the rappers he dissed, the most memorable response came from Jay-Z. Jay-Z's words were few but powerful. Jay-Z's 17-word response helped launch 50 Cent's career. You may remember them from the album *Vol. 3: Life and Times of S. Carter*.

> *"Go against*
>
> *Jigga yo' ass is*
>
> *dense I'm*
>
> *about a dollar.*

What the fuck

is 50 Cents?"

That bar was one of the greatest lines in a battle rap to show superiority and dominance. I remember hearing that line and wondering what 50 Cent was thinking of going against the big fish, the king of New York, the man who calls himself "HOVA." It all made sense as I grew older. 50 Cent understood the power of response. A reply transfers energy from one person to another through a series or episode of verbal exchanges. 50 Cent claimed victory by moving on. He simply called out enough people of influence until they all responded to him. His shit-talking tactic worked for him at the cost of relationships. The more people he called out, the more people he had a chance that would mention his name. The more people said his name, the more famous he became. The more famous he became, the more he pushed his agenda, which did not revolve around battling rappers but becoming an entrepreneur.

Be careful and consider who you respond to when others are talking bad about you. You can transfer power and energy for them to become more significant than they were supposed to be. Pay attention to the motive of the person speaking up about you. Ask yourself a few questions.

- Are they a friend?

- Do they have my best interest?

- Do their words hurt me?

- Are they attacking me or helping me?

- How do I feel after hearing their words?

You must control your thoughts and decide what you will do when someone's words enter your ears and touch your heart. Jay-Z could have not responded like the other rappers and ultimately would have ruined 50 Cent's career. I am sure ego played a considerable role in Jay-Z's response. One might say that writing a 17-word reaction was nothing compared to all the songs he wrote about Nas. The lack of words showed the lack of respect for 50 Cent and how little a factor he considered 50 to be. However, if you are the man or woman you say you are, think about who and what you spend your time on. The upside was clearly for 50 Cent while Jay-Z received little to no benefit. 50 Cent achieved his goal, but he did not stop there. The next summer, he dropped a song titled "Be a Gentleman," which was aimed at Jay-Z again. Jay-Z did not respond. Now, let's look at the power of silence and how you can effectively talk shit without saying one word.

Talking Shit in Silence

After an intense meeting with an employee, my mentor called me into her office. The employee and I had gone back and forth about why the employee was being addressed for their performance. My goal was to have the employee take ownership of their poor performance. I continued to grow frustrated that there was no ownership being taken, so I continued to press the issue. We were wasting air arguing over something that had facts associated with it.

As soon as I heard her say, "Michael, come to my office and let's talk," I knew I did not perform well. Her voice tone sounded like when your father or mother had read your progress report before you got home from school. I walked into her office, hoping, praying, and wishing that she would say I had done a good job. Nope. That did not happen. She explained how I got too emotionally involved in the meeting and how I allowed the employee to make their problem my problem.

I attempted to speak to defend myself and was abruptly cut off. She said, "Seriously, are you going to make an excuse right now?" Perhaps this was not the best time to talk my shit. My mentor explained that I do not have to respond to everything someone says. In her words, "Michael, you do not have to comment on everything that said in the room. You have facts. It is not your job to prove the facts but rather present them and hold others accountable. If you keep going back and forth with someone, the nature of the meeting changes from the topic at hand and turns into the back and forth everyone is experiencing."

My mind was blown. Where I come from, the more someone talks, the more you talk. The louder someone gets, the louder you get. Yup, you guessed right if you thought *Michael must be from New Jersey.*

My mentor shared that there is power in silence. She went on to explain how silence can control a room. The light bulb over my head got brighter and brighter as she spoke life into me. This was a tool I needed in my toolbox of effective communication.

"Imagine if you did not respond to the comments about the facts the employee was disputing." She went on, "Allow the facts to be what they are. You are not going to get anywhere arguing with people in life." She recalled the employee challenging me and asked, "What if you never responded? What if you just sat there and looked at the employee in silence, blinking, waiting for time to pass in silence before moving on to the next topic?"

I thought about it. She had done just that to me by posing a question and not speaking. I entered my headspace to search for a response. The air became dense, and I felt awkward. I then realized that there is power in silence. Talking shit does not always require you to yell, cry, or even speak. The art of talking shit in silence can be more powerful than talking shit out loud.

I was so impressed by the learnings that I could not wait to try it. Unfortunately, my wife was the first person to get it. Many of you know that you must have facts on top of facts if you will prove your wife wrong. I was ready. I had all the points a man needs to utilize this technique. I was ready. My wife questioned me about whether I thought something I did was right or wrong.

Yes, we have all been there. I was prepared, though. I shared facts

about my rationale, and my wife rechallenged me. I stared at her,

blinked multiple times, and said nothing. She grew more

frustrated, and I started to laugh inside because I was "winning"

the conversation without talking. I was talking shit in silence. I

then transitioned to the next topic she wanted to discuss, and she

had a look on her face like she wanted to drop kick me like a

soccer goalie after saving a goal. Men, I do not recommend this.

Use this tactic with caution. Also, please do not say, "Michael told

me to do this." I am just sharing an example of how effective this

could be—wink, wink, wink.

The effectiveness of not speaking must be used when it's

appropriate. Often, people talk too much and lose their audience

or the validity of the point they are trying to make. Listen more

and speak less. Jay-Z's first response was minimal words. His

second response was more powerful than the first because he did

not respond at all. Not responding to those who are not on your page is a powerful way to talk your shit without ever opening your

mouth.

Inter-Generational Communication

Times change. When times change, the preferred way of communication changes. Often, we find ourselves struggling to communicate with each other, especially when an older person and a younger person speak. The generational gaps have proven to be a setback in most instances where collaboration is needed.

The Greatest Generation (Traditionalists) 1922-1945

- Respect Authority

- Work comes before fun

- Rule followers

- Lead with control

- Prefer written communication

- No News is good news

Baby Boomer 1946-1964

- Workaholics

- Want high quality in their services and products

- Working as a team is relevant

- Prefer to communicate in person

- One on one meetings are preferred

- Let them know their contribution is needed

- Love to be rewarded with money

- Titles mean a lot to them

- Like to talk more about their work than their personal lives at home

Generation X 1965-1980

- Want structure

- Want direction

- Skeptical of the status quo

- View everyone as being the same

- Doesn't mind being challenged

- Communicate directly to them

- Prefer communication immediately after an event and not let time past

- Likes feedback

- Prefers to talk about personal and professional lives

Millennials 1981-1996

- Wonder about what is next

- Entrepreneurial

- Goal-Oriented

- Feel comfortable multitasking

- Prefer to communicate electronically (Text messages, social media post)

- Prefer their work to be meaningful

- Rely on continual feedback

- Thrive on teams with other bright, creative people.

Generation Z 1997 – 2012

- Does not remember the world without the internet

- Entrepreneurial Spirit

- Diverse and feel positive about diversity

- Less religious identification

- Blurry Lines/Vision – public and private have been blurred by social media

- Lonely – less face-to-face interaction due to increased social media activity

- Personalization – used to having things personalized like music playlist to news feed products

While the communication styles may vary among the generations, there are some foundational things that all ages prefer.

- Respect

- Structure

- Loyalty

- Feedback

- Trust

- Courtesy

Keeping the previously mentioned things in mind when communicating will allow you to communicate across generations effectively. Understanding the preferences of the different ages will enable you to understand what to do to communicate effectively.

This information is most important in the work environment. For example, if a Gen Xer is worried about structure and a Millennial is concerned about what next, how would you communicate this to satisfy communication to both groups in the workplace? If you are a Gen X leader, you may get frustrated with a Millennial. Millennials will ask what's next before you finish putting the structure together to share with the team. This may also happen in the home. If a Gen Xer is working on a home plan regarding chores, the millennial may feel the house is disorganized and lose trust in the parent. Open communication and transparency are key when communicating across generations. Suppose people are invited into the process and kept well informed of the plan. In that case, the likelihood of communication breakdown is low.

Also, understand that the year one is born may not align with their communication style. For example, I was born in 1984 but raised by my grandmother, who is a traditionalist. This makes my communication style somewhat of a hybrid of a Baby Boomer and a Millennial.

No matter what generation you are from, be respectful and courteous. We all have room to learn from each other. If you want to communicate across generations effectively, listen with an ear to learn. No generation is better than the other. Remember that each generation was raised by the previous generation.

Nonverbal Communication

Growing up in New Jersey, I was accustomed to communicating with facial expressions and hand gestures. I often must remind myself that I am not in New Jersey when I am in the corporate office. In Corporate America, the primary mode of communication is words. There is power in nonverbal communication.

Have you ever been playing with your siblings and could feel your parents communicating to you even though you were not looking at them? I remember my older brother and me sitting on the church bench down the row from my Grandmother like yesterday. My brother and I would flick each other's ears, shoot spitballs at each other, and make funny faces to see who would laugh out loud and get in trouble. We did all of this while the service was taking place. It did not matter if the preacher was preaching or if the choir was singing. We were trying to have fun and stay awake. Now and then, I would feel my grandmother's eyes peering at my brother and me as we did childish things and low key embarrassed her during church services. Her eyes would stare at us with such intent that we would slow down and eventually stop what we were doing. Once we stopped, we knew that we then had to look her way and make eye contact to acknowledge that we were in trouble. Our heads lowered and eyes raised like the puppy who just had an accident on the floor were our attempt to ask for forgiveness and mercy.

The puppy-dog look never worked, but we tried it every time. There were never words exchanged, but our postures and facial expressions clearly showed that we were scared. Now, as for my grandmother, her eyebrows raised at each corner, tilted towards the center, wrinkles across her forehead, lips scrunched up as if she smelled something bad. A finger pointing at us that seemed ten feet long accompanied by the head shake of shame. Mentally I could hear her saying, "You better cut it out, or I would cut you out." Yes, you heard it right. Often, we interpret nonverbal communication based on previous encounters or perception. In this case, I knew from similar situations that we were in big trouble when we got home.

Nonverbal communication refers to facial expressions, gestures made with your body, tone of voice, and eye contact or lack thereof. Nonverbal communication can supplement your verbal communication and often can be perceived as a more potent form of communication. Nonverbal communication can serve as a primary or supplementary form of communication. There are five roles nonverbal communication can play.

Contradiction

Have you ever said something with your mouth and communicated something different with your face? Okay, I guess I will be the person to say it. Have you ever seen an ugly baby? Now, answer this question honestly. When many of us see an ugly baby, we will say things like, "Oh, wow. Look at the baby;" "Oh, that's a baby baby;" or "Aw, look at the outfit." We have all been there. The problem with this is that we often fall victim to poor nonverbal communication called contradiction. The words say one thing, and facial expression or body language says something else. We tell on ourselves. The words say, "Look at the baby," and the facial expression conveys, "Look at the ugly baby." **Contradiction** occurs when the verbal message does not align with the nonverbal message. Avoid this at all costs. Perhaps just say congratulations and nod a few times at their new baby addition.

Repetition

Active listening plays a massive role in repetition. Have you ever been in a conversation with someone, and they nod their head every time you make a solid point? You know the person who leans in to hear what you are saying, and at the end of each break, they slowly nod their head in a way to agree with what you said. This is an example of repetition. **Repetition** takes place when someone is communicating nonverbally by repeating what they are doing. Repetition strengthens the message received or delivered.

Accenting

Coming from New Jersey, I would say we are notorious for accenting conversations nonverbally with noises made by our hands and feet. You may have seen this occur when someone is in an intense discussion and then slams his or her hands on the table to make a point. The point could be made without the hands banging on the table; however, the slamming accents the point being made with more authority and commands attention.

I am by no way encouraging you to slap and or slam things around you to prove a point. I am bringing to your awareness that there may be an appropriate time to accent a conversation with nonverbal accenting. Choose wisely if you will accent a conversation. People will often not remember what you said, but they will remember what you did and how you made them feel. **Accenting** assists in underlining the verbal message.

Complementing

Complementing is important to nonverbal communication because it can also reinforce a message and positively impact the message. Have you ever had a boss tell you that you did a good job? How did you feel? Have you ever had a boss tell you that you did a good job and then follow it up with a few pats on the shoulder? How did you feel? This tactic is not for people who are not touchy-feely. Complementing can help reassure people that the communication shared is genuine. As a nurse, I would often use this technique on my patients when I wanted them to know I would be there for them. I would simply let them know I am there for them and place my hand on their shoulder. The shoulder was my safe spot. Be sure when complimenting that you utilize the most appropriate form of nonverbal communication for the situation. Do not pat someone on the butt to say "good job" in the church as if you are on the football team. The two just do not go together. **Complementing** is the process of touching someone during communication to reinforce the message.

Substitution

Instead of speaking, sometimes you must utilize facial expressions to show how you feel. Substitute words for facial expressions when you cannot find the words to use. For example, if someone told you something important to them, and you do not know how to respond, show your empathy through your facial expression. **Substitution** takes place when you replace verbal comments with physical facial gestures.

Source: The Importance of Effective Communication, Edward G. Wertheim, Ph.D.

https://www.helpguide.org/articles/relationships-communication/nonverbal-communication.htm

Insecurities and Speaking Up

Insecurities rob people every day from living their best life. Outer appearance has become more important than intellect by far since the implementation of social media. Speaking up means nothing if you don't look the part or act the part. You will always struggle with speaking up if you do not build self-confidence and reassure yourself that you are a badass no matter what others think of you. Own your look. Own your imperfections. Work on the things you need to work on to achieve the level of success you deserve. You must be able to talk shit, so those around you hear your story and get to know you. Be true to who you are. If you are a suburban kid from an affluent neighborhood, be you. If you are an adult from the hood, be you. It doesn't matter where you are from; what matters is being true to who you are. The kid from a wealthy neighborhood may have the same insecurities the poor kid has from the hood. Your DNA genetic makeup is what it is. Either way, you need to speak up, and that won't happen until you address your insecurities. Addressing insecurities requires self-reflection.

Look in the mirror. Ask yourself, "Am I ugly? Do I have a nasty attitude? Am I a jerk? What am I good at? What am I great at? What makes me uniquely different from others?" Once you ask those questions, answer them, and address them. This process will establish the foundation for being able to talk your shit. You will only be able to effectively speak up about things you are 100% confident in.

I know this is not easy. It's not easy because who wants to look at the "ugly you." Social media has programmed many of us to portray the cool you. Displaying insecurities isn't a crime if you are working on them. I have more respect for the transparent person talking shot than the hypocrite who talks a lot of shit while living a foul life.

Remember, the caption means nothing if the picture doesn't match the words. Build your self-confidence today. Deal with yourself the way you need to if you are serious about being

heard.

Communication and Relationship

Relationship Talking

Who is your favorite shit talker? You know who they are. The person that speaks with confidence, that knows it all but also openly admits when they mess up. Some people may say Gary Vaynerchuck or better known as Gary V for his in your face approach to deliver a message. Some of you may say your mother or father when it was time for you to be disciplined. I always wondered where they learned how to speak to me and my siblings in such a way to make us listen without touching us. Perhaps it was the bully in school who would deliver a message in such a way that scared everyone in the classroom. Talking shit is amazing when it is done with the right motive to ensure a message is delivered appropriately. Typically, your favorite shit talker is the person you mimic when in when building a relationship in some form or fashion. Theres a difference between running game and talking bullshit than talking the right shit and building a relationship.

Running Game is Bullshit

Growing up "running game on a girl" was one of the most celebrated things discussed among friends. As time moved on the ladies understood the benefits of "running game" on men and quickly became better at it. Nonetheless running game is bullshit. The journey to achieve and conquer someone mentally is what keeps people doing this over and over. Sometimes this can come at a financial cost or mental cost of those running the game or those having game ran on them.

You may have heard this before, Wow you look amazing, I am so attracted to your mind, It's like you understand me in a world where no one understands me, I see you for who you are and what you stand for, I could never replace someone like you in my life and blah blah blah blah blah. Run and run fast from anyone using these terms. They are out for one thing and one thing only which is your soul!

What was your state of mind?

_____

_____

_____

_____

_____

_____

Did someone tragic happen to you? If so what?

_____

_____

_____

_____

_____

What would you do differently to avoid being played?

_____

_____

_____

_____

_____

The sound of being appreciated and accepted sooths the mind in the most troubling times. Many people seek love for affection, protection, and acceptance. However, relationship building as it pertains to love must rely on transparency, loyalty, and honesty. No one will ever achieve all three in a relationship which means forgiveness plays a huge role in moving forward. Lets not mistaken forgiving someone as the same as continuously allowing someone to play with your emotions intentionally or unintentionally. Protect your heart at all times from bullshit. In order to effectively talk shit in a relationship you mut first understand the languages of love.

Relationship Etiquette

I highly recommend reading a book titled The Five Love Languages by Gary Chapman. Gary explains in his book that there are five ways to express and receive love. After reading it I see it like this, just because you like a color doesn't mean your partner likes a color. The goal is for you to communicate in a way your partner will understand. Many times, we fail to do this because we naturally communicate in a way that we feel we would like to be communicated to. In order to effectively communicate in a relationship, you must first listen. Once you listen you must then repeat what you heard to determine what steps you will take next.

My wife shared with me that she did not feel comfortable driving small cars because her first care was an SUV. I immediately wanted to speak her language, so I purchased her an Excursion. I thought that I heard her say she wanted a big SUV. Many years later my wife shared it was hard to keep her SUV clean because

she was the parent that took the kids to school and home daily.
She shared that we used her SUV for hauling the dogs around and
picking up large item things needed around the house. I struggled
with listening to her because I felt I got it right the first time by
getting her what she wanted. As I realized I got it wrong, I ended
up purchasing her a two-seater Mercedes Benz convertible. My
rationale was that the sports car would not get dirty because it
only has room for two people and the kids were too young to ride
in the front seat. I was so excited I surprised her with it on her
birthday along with a dinner to a five-star restaurant and a
shopping spree in LA. The day went well. As time went by I
noticed my wife would not drive the car. I asked her what was
wrong, and she said "nothing". Nothing then turned into a reason
which included she could not take the kids with her. I became
angry because she was not understanding that I heard her and got
her what I thought she wanted. My feelings were hurt. I traded in
my dream car and brought her the car I thought she wanted of
her dreams.

Fast forward a few years the car continued to sit, and I refused to start it up or encourage her to drive it. After reading the Five Love Languages I realized that I was talking to her in my love language which is receiving gifts. I started to discuss the love languages with her and realized her love language was words of affirmation and quality time. Wow did I ever blow it! I purchased her a car with confirming this is what she wanted (Twice) and then took quality time away from her by getting her a two-seater that does not allow for a mother to ride around with her kids. I was clearly the loser in this situation. As I realized what her love language was, I simply asked her what is your dream car. My wife answered with a huge smile on her face and told me it was a Range Rover. I told her to tell me about it. She shared all the specs she wanted and the whole nine yards. I apologized for buying her the wrong car twice and that I should have simply asked her what she wanted. I am sure when I get the next car, It will be the correct one for sure.

5 Love Languages

Lets Take a Quick look at the 5 love languages.

Words of Affirmation – Encourage, Affirm, Appreciate,

Empathize, and listen actively.

Acts of Service- Use action phrases like "I'll Help "so they know

you want and are supporting them.

Receiving Gifts- give thoughtful gifts and remember that small

things matter

Quality Time – uninterrupted focused time. One on one time.

Physical Touch – use body language to emphasize love (Hugs,

Kisses, ect)

If someone tells you they love you and they do not speak your

love language they are lying. If someone says they love you within

a few moments of meeting you, they are more than likely lying as

well. Many people look for love they way they want to be loved

but true love is about giving unconditionally to someone you've

learned to understand, care about, and ride out life with. I highly recommend reading the Five Love Languages so that you can

speak up effectively in your relationships.

What's your love language? _____

What's your partners love language? _____

Women Talk Shit Too

The real beauty of a woman isn't the curves in her hips or the roundness of her breast or how perfect her smile is. The beauty of a woman is her voice. The sounds that come out of a woman's mouth that displays wisdom and understanding. The sounds that came out when they started advocating for justice when injustice was present. The voice of women speaking up for equality. The voice of the women who for other women who have been raped and molested. I love when women talk shit. They have a way of uniting and getting things done.

History has shown the power of women speaking up over and over. Let's take a trip down memory lane and chronicle some stories about women speaking up and talking their shit.

Examples of Women that Spoke up
Ruth Bader Ginsburg, a.k.a. Notorious RBG
History

Ruth's claim to fame was all about speaking up. First and foremost, Ruth did the work to qualify to have the voice to speak up. Ruth graduated first in her class at Columbia Law School. Due to discrimination, she was not able to find a job. She then worked as a law professor. Ruth began to be an advocate for women's legal rights. Ruth ultimately served as an associate justice of the supreme court in the United States from 1993-2020. Ruth was the first Jewish woman and the second woman to serve on the Court.

Take some time to read the powerful quotes of the Notorious RBG

"Women belong in all places where decisions are being made. It shouldn't be that women are the exception."

"Don't be distracted by emotions like anger, envy, resentment,"

"These just zap energy and waste time."

"When a thoughtless or unkind word

is spoken, best tune out."

"Fight for the things that you care

about but do it in a way that will

lead others to join you."

Maya Angelou

History

Maya Angelou was a civil rights activist and poet. She published several books. Maya has received numerous awards and over 50 honorary degrees for the impact she had on society. Maya Angelou is well known for speaking up for women and black people. Her messages addressing racism, self-identity, and family were delivered with passion, truth, and love. Maya's transparency in her writing shares that she worked in the sex trade industry as a prostitute for lesbians, having kids, and experienced injustice. Her powerful delivery helped many people rise above their circumstances. Angelou received the Presidential Medal of

Freedom from President Barack Obama and won three Grammys for her spoken word albums.

Below are a few quotes from Maya.

"If you're always trying to be normal, you will never know how amazing you can be."

"I've learned that people will forget what you said, people will forget what you did, but people will never forget how you made them feel."

"We delight in the beauty of the butterfly but rarely admit the changes it has gone through to achieve that beauty."

"If you don't like something, change it. If you can't change it, change your attitude."

"If I am not good to myself, how can

I expect anyone else to be good to

me?"

"When someone shows you who

they are, believe them the first

time."

Emmeline Pankhurst

History

Emmeline was not one to shy away from speaking up. As a British political activist, she simply called for action in the early 1900s when a woman's voice was no near as powerful as it is today. She founded the women's social and political union campaign for women's parliamentary vote in Edwardian Britain. Her motto was "Deeds, not words." I would translate this as "Don't talk about it. Be about it." Her speaking up landed her in prison 13 times. Her efforts included advocating for equal pay for equal work, equal job opportunities, and equal marriage laws.

Quotes from Emmeline

"I would rather be a rebel than a

slave."

"Men make the moral code, and

they expect women to accept it.

They have decided that it is entirely

right and proper for men to fight for

their liberties and their rights, but

that it is not right and proper for

women to fight for theirs."

"There is something that

Governments care for far more than

human life, and that is the security

of property, and so it is through

property that we shall strike the

enemy. Be militant each in your own

way. I incite this meeting to

rebellion."

"Justice and judgment lie often a

world apart."

"It is obvious to you that the struggle

will be an unequal one, but I shall

make it - I shall make it as long as I

have an ounce of strength left in me

or any life left in me."

Florence Nightingale

History

I may be partial to picking Florence due to being a nurse, but I love her history and what she stood for. Being a black male nurse was made possible because of Florence's ability to speak up and set a standard that did not have a gender bias. Florence was the founder of modern nursing. Florence trained nurses in a wartime setting as well as organized care for wounded soldiers. Florence is also known for abolishing prostitution laws that were harsh on women. She also focused on expanding the acceptable forms of participation of females in the workforce.

Quotes By Florence

"I attribute my success to this - I never gave or took any excuse."

"Live life when you have it. Life is a splendid gift – there is nothing small about it."

"Wise and humane management of the patient is the best safeguard against infection."

"I do see the difference now between me and other men. When a disaster happens, I act, and they make excuses."

"I think one's feelings waste themselves in words; they ought all to be distilled into actions which bring results."

Malala Yousafzai

History

Malala is a Pakistani activist for female education. Being an activist in a country where you could be persecuted is a risky job. Malala is the youngest receiver of the Nobel peace prize, age 17. Her advocacy took place where girls were banned from attending school. Her advocacy turned into an international movement. A Taliban gunman shot her because she spoke up for girls' right to an education.

Quotes by Malala

"So let us wage a glorious struggle against illiteracy, poverty, and terrorism, let us pick up our books and our pens. They are the most powerful weapons.

"Dear friends, on 9 October 2012, the Taliban shot me on the left side of my forehead. They shot my

friends, too. They thought that the

bullets would silence us, but they

failed. And out of that silence came

thousands of voices. The terrorists

thought they would change my aims

and stop my ambitions. But nothing

changed in my life except this:

weakness, fear, and hopelessness

died. Strength, power, and courage

was born. I am the same Malala. My

ambitions are the same. My hopes

are the same."

"I used to think I had to wait to be

an adult to lead. But I've learned

that even a child's voice can be

heard around the world."

"Often, we think we are too young,

or our ideas may not work, and we

need to grow up to bring change. I

just say no. Whatever you want to

do now, you can do it now."

"The world needs leadership based

on serving humanity — not based on

how many weapons you have."

"We need to encourage girls that

their voice matters. I think there are

hundreds and thousands of Malala's

out there."

Sojourner Truth
History

Sojourner, born Isabella "Belle" Baumfree in the late 1700s, fought for the freedom of slaves and women's rights. As a black woman, she was not considered human or a citizen. Her stance was revolutionary for all black people. She was born into slavery and escaped with her daughter to freedom in 1826. She was also the first black woman to win a case against a white man in court as she fought for her son's custody. She helped recruit black troops for the union army. Her speech titled "Ain't I a Woman?" was revolutionary. It focused on women's physical and intellectual strength.

Sojourner Truth Quotes

"Truth is powerful, and it prevails."

"If women want any rights more than they's got, why don't they just take them, and not be talking about it."

"I am not going to die; I'm going home like a shooting star.

"That man over there says that women need to be helped into carriages, and lifted over ditches, and to have the best place everywhere. Nobody ever helps me

into carriages, or over mud-puddles,

or gives me any best place! And ain't

I a woman? Look at me! Look at my

arm! I have ploughed and planted,

and gathered into barns, and no

man could head me! And ain't I a

woman? I could work as much and

eat as much as a man - when I could

get it - and bear the lash as well!

And ain't I a woman? I have borne

five children and seen most all sold

off to slavery, and when I cried out

with my mother's grief, none but

Jesus heard me! And ain't I a

woman?"

"If the first woman God ever made

was strong enough to turn the world

upside down all alone, these women

together ought to be able to turn it

back and get it right side up again!

And now they is asking to do it, the

men better let them."

"Let others say what they will of the

efficacy of prayer, I believe in it, and

I shall pray. Thank God! Yes, I shall

always pray,"

"You may hiss as much as you

please, but women will get their

rights anyway."

As you can see, a woman's voice is powerful. Women can join forces for the greater good of humanity.

Which one of the previously mentioned women inspired you?

_____

_____

_____

_____

Why did they inspire you?

_____

_____

_____

_____

What are you going to do differently to impact humanity
based on their inspiration significantly?

_____

_____

_____

_____

Name three more women that inspire you from History.

_____

_____

_____

Name two women in your life that inspire you.

_____

_____

_____

What have they done to inspire you?

_____

_____

_____

_____

Email, text, or call the women in your life that inspire you and share the impact they have had on your life.

Write down who the person was and their response.

Name _____

Response: _____

Name _____

Response: _____

Name _____

Response: _____

Shitty Conversations – How to Have an Effective Difficult Conversation

By the time the conversation ended, I felt disrespect and unappreciated. I questioned everything I did. Was I not good enough? Was I not educated enough? Was I too black? Maybe I wasn't strong enough. My leadership had been questioned. I was kicked off the team. This conversation sounded familiar from when I was in the military. During my evaluation, I was told I was not a good enough leader to receive the highest remarks on my evaluation. I thought I had overcome that part of my life. I questioned if my humbleness was being exploited. Was I too nice? You know, being nice to the point where people don't think you have a backbone. It was a tough conversation. I was told I wasn't a team player. I was told I wasn't contributing. I was told if I was not going to contribute, then I should get off the team. Before I could reply, I was kicked off the team. Fuck! I didn't sign up for this bullshit. I didn't sign up to be disrespected. I signed up to be great and help people. I was told I was pretty much a waste of time and effort.

This occurred in a meeting I had with a well-respected mentor after debriefing about a team meeting we were to lead together. I had my reasons as to why I was quiet in the room while the meeting was happening. However, that did not matter to my mentor. Nor was what I wasn't doing and how I wasn't helping. Difficult conversations are a must if you are going to be able to talk your shit.

My mentor had watched me display this behavior for months. Their evidence was irrefutable, and the comments were piercing. The hand gestures sent my emotions into a vulnerable uproar. My mentor had this all planned out. They were ready to talk shit to me to get the point across. My feelings got the best of me. It was not because my mentor didn't want me on the team. It was not because I was being questioned, nor was it because I was called a few names along the way. My emotions got the best of me because someone I respected rejected me. Rejection took me to a time when my grandmother and aunt raised me because my parents did not take care of me. As children, we don't always understand why our parents do what they do, but all I knew was that I felt rejected.

Managing your emotions during a difficult conversation is challenging. Triggers will send you into a headspace that will make you see and hear things that are never being said. To effectively talk shit in a difficult conversation, you must first watch your opposition. Study their behaviors to determine if what you will say is real or full of emotions. Study the person you will talk to and ask them questions to understand their train of thought before having a difficult conversation. My mentor shit on me, for lack of better words. They effectively reached deep into my soul. They made me question myself and caused me to have a difficult conversation.

One would think the difficult conversation would have been with my mention. NOPE! The problematic discussion was with my mentor's boss. Before you say, "No," I wasn't there to snitch. I was there to make my next move and prove my worth.

Before the conversation, I knew I had to have my shit together because I was sure the big boss knew I had been kicked off the team because of my poor leadership. I studied the big boss's keys to success, which included hard work and no excuses. When I called the big boss, I knew they did not care about being kicked off the team more than they cared about my lack of hard work and overcoming excuses. The phone was answered with "Hiiiiiiiiiiii Michael." It was the tone your mother or grandmother uses when you are in trouble.

I quickly jumped into the conversation, thoroughly composed and free of emotions. I was ready to talk my shit. I started by saying, "I'm sure you heard what happened, and I'm not here to refute that. I am here to make it happen."

The big boss said, "Tell me more."

I then began to share my strengths and how I could assist in specific areas. I created a new role. The big boss agreed I was the man for the job. My shit-talking was so convincing that I was only lightly reprimanded for my lack of engagement. The big boss simply said, "Okay, tighten up. Show me what you got."

Wow. A simple "show me what you" got coupled with "you are off my team" from my mentor turned me into a successful leader. I moved with purpose. I executed with focus. I won the "people's vote," which won my mentor's and big boss's respect.

Having difficult conversations are painful, yet they are needed. Difficult conversations open opportunities for improvement and understanding. The purpose of having a difficult conversation is for people to either agree or to agree to disagree peacefully. Everyone is uniquely made, and one of the biggest frustrations in life is trying to get others to understand why your brain thinks the way it does. The answer is simple. Your mind thinks the way it does because it's your brain. More importantly, your life experiences cause your brain to remember or recall history, which formulated your response. Overcoming this to have a clear conscience requires a high-level EQ around self-awareness.

EQ is what's needed to have effective difficult conversations.

The Conversation That Never Happened

It's story time. Follow me.

I told them my next move as if they had already heard the story. Their eyes quickly started closing as they tried to recall the conversation. One eye even started twitching. I dismissed the signs of facial expressions. I was talking my shit about my next moves that involved them. The plan was laid out. I knew what I had committed to doing mentally and physically. My voice got stronger and louder the more I realized the person wasn't on my page. I mean, we did talk about this, right? Right? Hold up, did we talk about this? Yea, we did. It was on ummmmmmmmm. Damn, I can't remember, but I remember. Have you ever been in a situation where you remember what you can't remember? Okay, I must be crazy. Nah. Not me. I'm usually right. I'm generally excellent with communication. Well, guess what they said. "You never discussed this with me."

"SHIT!" I thought. I couldn't remember what I remembered. I had to admit they were right. *Nah. Forget that. My plan is solid, so I'll dismiss what never happened.* The conversation started to escalate because my shit-talking had devolved into bullshit even though my plan was solid. I had to look in the mirror and admit I was wrong because I thought I had a conversation about something I thought I remember.

Frequently, highly productive people will have internal mental conversations with others. This mostly happens when you have a mental conversation with someone you know well and can guess what they would say. Closing the loop on mental discussions is vital to everyone involved in decision-making. You may have experienced this with your best friend, parents, spouse, or boss. We can become so busy that the time we have each day doesn't seem like enough. Our goal is to be as efficient as possible.

Let's not confuse this with habitual liars and manipulators who say they had a conversation with you for their self-gain. The critical observation is usually self-gain. They will look you in your face and talk bullshit. Beware of these people. They are cancerous and dangerous because they will manipulate you and make you feel sad about their situation. They often play the victim in the situation. Nonetheless, stay focused on what you know is true.

When you find yourself in a situation where you thought you had a conversation and did not, here is how you address it.

Stop trying to get your point across. Ask the person do they remember the conversation. Look at their eyes. You will notice one or two things. Either their eyes will have an appearance of searching and ending up with nothing, or their eyes will look you fiercely in your eyes and state no. Either way, you must trust your gut. Gather your thoughts. Apologize and lean into a productive discussion to reach agreements. Try it.

- Do you remember?

- Are you sure?

- Well, pardon me because I thought we had this conversation.

- Let's move forward and talk about it now if you have time.

- I'm willing to put my ideas on hold until we reach an agreement that will benefit both of us.

Following this process will decrease frustrations and increase communication. The end goal is to learn how to communicate effectively. We often lose family and friends due to conversations that mentally happened and never actually physically happened. Life is too short. Humble yourself. Be honest and make the right decision. Your reputation is on the line. It's up to you to protect it. If you don't, people will see you as unapproachable and hard to communicate with. Agreements are key.

I was screaming at the top of my lungs how wrong they were. How foul they were. How inconsiderate they were. Who would waste my time and use me to get ahead? As they shouted "fuck you," my ears received it. My soul declined it. My heart ate it. And my mouth returned it. "Nooooooo FUCK YOU!" Since this was an argument, I had to one-up the "fuck you" by adding "bitch" on the end. FUCK YOU BITCH! Ahhhhh. The battle was almost won. I thought to myself, don't let up now. Put the nail in the coffin. So I did and hung up the phone and blocked the number. I blocked our social media connections and exhaled. Did I feel good? No. Did I win the argument? I think I did because I cursed more and was louder and more passionate about the topic. I hung the phone up, so I guessed this was what victory felt like.

As I look back at the situation, I reflect on how I could have handled it better. All my Spidey senses were firing, and my stomach started turning. The light bulb turned on, and I realized I lost the fight. The "petty" me reminded the "mature" me that It was needed. An internal conversation between Mr. Petty and Mr. Mature quickly escalated to a bottom line, which consisted of me realizing I needed to handle disagreements differently.

Twitter Fingers Race, Religion, Politics

Opinions are everywhere. Everyone has one about race, religion, and politics. The areas have been made grey over the years. Race has become a topic of discussion for various reasons, including inclusion, separation, segregation, and racism. Religion is at the forefront of a debate regarding where you go when you die and moral values. Politics are even more complicated. It is driven by agreeing to disagree, standing for what you believe even when it doesn't align with others, and how governments should run things.

I woke up and decided to make a post about my political views on racism. It's social media. I have freedom of speech. I served my country in wartime, so technically, I could say what I want, correct? The notifications took off like a cheetah after a gazelle—Bing, bing, bing, bing, bing. The phone light repeated on and off like lightning on a stormy night. I swiped right and opened my phone to see what the fuss was about. Low and behold, it was about my political view on racism.

With no thought, I began to respond and defend my position. Just like anyone would with genuine beliefs. My comments were piercing and well written. Shutting down every "hater" was my goal. Before I knew it, I had spent about three hours laboring over my phone, engaging in social media arguing. I'm sure my blood pressure was up, and my pulse was through the roof. My family started to feel the effects of me being overwhelmed. I needed to talk to someone about the disrespect I was encountering. Over the next few hours, I stopped responding because I realized what I did and did not have power over. It is incredibly frustrating when you don't have control, and you have been fighting for something.

The definition of "to argue" is to give reasons for or against something. Unfortunately, the definition does not include possible side effects. You know the side effects announced at the end of medicine commercials. They sound something like, "This medication will help with your depression. You will be happy and thriving." This is then followed by a series of words warning you of how you may die or have diarrhea.

The definition of arguing should have the side effects listed first and then the meaning. I'm confident that many of us would change how we engage others if we knew the side effects. Arguing in an aggressive or exhausting manner can cause fatigue, depression, anger, loss of hope, and ultimately cost you a relationship you weren't ready to lose.

Both previous examples had me on edge. To effectively talk shit in an argument, you must first consider a few things.

Are you mentally stable? Be honest with yourself. Are you in a position to argue with anyone, or are you suffering from emotional takeover, biased viewpoints, depression, PTSD, or maybe even a lack of maturity?

Next, considered your audience. Do not just consider the person you are speaking to. Also, consider the people around you that see and hear you talking up. To be free and speak up comes at a cost. A mature person will do a risk assessment.

As the question, does the risk outweigh the benefits? This is a military approach to war. Before entering a conflict, military officials will do a risk assessment. Ask yourself if arguing will be worth putting your health and reputation at risk. At the end of the day, if you don't have your health, you do not have anything. If you don't protect your reputation, you leave it to others to justify your greatness. Once you've considered the risk write them down.

Writing the risks will help you determine what you are willing to lose for the argument. Is it worth it? You may not realize what you're losing until you review the benefits.

Consider the benefits of what you will gain by engaging in an argument. Many of us just want to be right. We want to "win" and stand on top of whoever came for us. No one wakes up with the mindset to lose an argument. The benefits must be honorable and full of integrity

You must be ready for the consequences of whatever you decide to do. Effectively talking shit in an argument boils down to one thing and one thing only. Does the benefit outweigh the risk of you losing something or someone you value?

Let's reflect on a past argument. Fill out the next sections and determine your effectiveness. Remember, the win isn't about making someone feel bad. Success is about helping the other person understand your perspective while minimizing hurt, pain, and miscommunication.

Write down the situation you argued about

_____

_____

_____

_____

_____

_____

_____

_____

_____

_____

_____

_____

Were you mentally stable to engage in an argument? If not, explain why.

_____

_____

_____

_____

_____

_____

_____

_____

_____

_____

_____

If not, what things do you need to work on?

_____

_____

_____

_____

_____

_____

_____

_____

_____

_____

_____

What were the risks associated with arguing?

_____

_____

_____

_____

_____

_____

_____

_____

_____

_____

_____

What were the benefits associated with arguing?

_____

_____

_____

_____

_____

_____

_____

_____

Did the benefits outweigh the risks? And if so explain why or why not.

_____

_____

_____

_____

_____

_____

_____

_____

_____

_____

_____

Was there any miscommunication? If so, what was it?

_____

_____

_____

_____

_____

_____

_____

_____

_____

_____

Were you prepared for the consequences?

_____

_____

_____

_____

_____

_____

_____

_____

_____

_____

What would you do differently?

_____

_____

_____

_____

_____

_____

_____

_____

_____

_____

Taking time to write things down helps your emotions align with your mind. The process of writing things down slows down your thoughts so that they become more evident. Writing things down also holds you accountable.

Argue less and listen more.

Beyond the Interview

Speaking up always has a risk associated with it. It's up to you to determine if you're going to shoot your shot and go after what you want or need. I remember the day like it was yesterday. It was over 115 degrees outside in Iraq. Yes. Iraq. I was serving my country when the senior chief called me to meet with him. I walked into the room, confident knowing I was about to receive my evaluation. My confidence came from my recollection of memories of things I did regarding my performance. I ran the most efficient team with the highest survival rate in a war zone. I received a three-star general's coin for extraordinary leadership. Everyone wanted to work on my team. This evaluation was a no brainer.

I eased into my seat with a smile on my face. The senior chief went through the evaluation. At the end of it, he stated, "You almost had it." He meant I almost performed well enough to receive the highest mark for promotion. My smiling face filled with confusion. How could I not receive the highest mark? I had college credits, a nursing license, and people survived at a higher

rate when my team provided their care. I let him finish explaining

why he decided I did not deserve the highest mark. As he finished,

I interrupted him and said, "Thank you for encouraging me to

leave the military where injustice is thriving because of people like

you." I let him know that I would now get out of the military and

be a great leader. I mean, after all, he stated I needed to work on

my leadership. I then let him know that he should remember me

one day because when he retires, he may meet me on the other

side of the table where I'm now in charge, and he is looking for a

job. The senior enlisted person behind him looked up at me with a

look of surprise and telling me to zip it up with his eyes. I was

talking my shit. This was fuel to my fire. I left that meeting

determined to succeed by any means necessary. As I left, multiple

factors went through my head. Was I a weak leader? Was he

discriminating against me because I was not his same race? The

others that received the high mark were of the same race as he

was. I replayed every warm and cold body that came through the doors that I treated. I recalled every conversation I had with the junior military personnel. I had no time to waste on things I had no control over. I immediately began to think about how to improve my leadership skills.

I transitioned out of the military and applied for multiple leadership positions. Little to my knowledge, what I did in the military meant nothing without a degree in the civilian world. How could I talk my shit in an interview if I didn't qualify to be invited to an interview? I went to school and grinded to accomplish what I needed.

The time was now. I had worked hard for this opportunity. I had put in many hours studying and graduating with multiple degrees. I sat in the waiting area with a pleasant lady. We exchanged a few words and smiled. The interviewer came to the waiting room and invited us both back to interview against each other. *Oh, shit*, I thought. I was just talking to the competition and didn't know it. I began to review my mental notes taken about the place where I wanted to work. I had done my research about the business and what areas they performed well in. I also low key interviewed some of the staff in passing by to see how their morale was. I understood the mission statement and vision statement. I just needed an opportunity to interview to show them I was the right person for the job.

The interview went well. I was confident. I know I outperformed my competition. It was just a matter of time before they would offer me the job. A week later, I reached out because I had not heard anything. The boss dropped a bomb on me. The boss shared they went with the other candidate because they had years of experience as a manager. My next move in this situation would determine my future. I thanked the boss for the opportunity. That night I went to sleep thinking about what I experienced. The next day I wrote an email to the interviewing team, thanking them for the opportunity and encouraging them to be great and perform well. I did not receive a response. I thought nothing of it until three weeks later the boss called me and stated the job was mine if I was still interested. I gladly accepted the position. Before the phone hung up, the boss shared that my email is what made them reconsider. My email. My email. My email. Wow. I was well on my way to being a great leader with this new opportunity. Stay tuned for my next book that focuses on decision making through inspired decision making.

Your degree gets you in the door. Your interview gets you a seat at the table. Your performance keeps your seat at the table.

Fast forward seven years, I find myself preparing for another position in leadership. After interviewing over 100 people, I was well in tune with what needs to happen in an interview. Here was another opportunity for me to talk my shit.

Interviewing for Success

Preparing to talk your shit in an interview requires a few things to be put in place if you are going to succeed. I've always told those around me that I could accept being rejected for a job if I was not the right fit. However, if I was being rejected or not considered because I did not qualify, I am at fault for that.

Education

To effectively talk shit in an interview, you must first have the education needed to qualify. As previously mentioned, I had the experience and not the formal education for the jobs I pursued. Could you imagine a pilot that never passed aviation school flying a plane? Let me rephrase the question. Would you let a surgeon operate on you if he or she never went to school to perform surgery? Education serves as a foundation for the knowledge needed to perform the job you are pursuing. Knowledge is power. Seek it and obtain it.

Once you've got the knowledge, work on gaining experience. Getting experience may be challenging, but you must seize every opportunity to get as much experience as you need. If you're interested in being a plumber and finished school but cannot find a job, reach out to plumbing companies to volunteer. Volunteering is better than doing nothing and then wondering why you haven't been invited to interview. Your volunteer hours will begin to count towards your experience.

As you complete the two previously mentioned things, research the company where you want to work. Find out what their mission statement and vision statement is. Find out how they are performing. What are they known for? What areas do they excel in? What areas of opportunity do they have? What's the morale of the employees? Finding all of this out will help you effectively interview.

Have Stories but Get to the Point.

Recall stories you may want to tell when answering questions at the interview. Share stories to appear human and relatable; however, do not get caught up telling the story. And don't forget to answer the question. Be sure your account is relevant to the question being asked.

Example:

Question: How do you like to be managed?

Answer: Being managed is ok, but I prefer to be led by leaders who have the employees' and the company's best interest at heart. I had a leader in the past that would make decisions about workflows based on employee morale, organizational

efficiency, and ensuring the customer was at the center of

decision making.

Now that you have your stories in line, it's time to look the

part.

Dressing for Success

The way you dress plays an essential role in your

confidence to deliver answers. Being well dressed sends a

statement to the potential employer. How you dress can affect

how you perform during your interview. Science says that the

clothes we wear affect our mood. Our behavior, attitude,

confidence, and the way we interact will also be affected. Your

goal is to dress appropriately for the job. Let your outfit speak for

itself before you open your mouth. There is no better feeling than

wearing a custom suit or an outfit that you picked. You must value

the opportunity to interview so much that you are willing to

spend the money needed to ensure you look and feel good.

What will you do differently during your next opportunity to interview for a position?

_____

_____

_____

_____

_____

_____

_____

_____

_____

_____

Agreements Start Somewhere

Where are we going to eat? This is how the infamous conversation starts in any relationship. When we ask this question at the beginning of the relationship, it's fun, engaging, and easy to find out what and where we want to eat. The friendly exchange of words comes at no cost to the relationship. It ends in an agreement where both people are usually satisfied. If the place you choose is not good, you will agree that you both did not pick a good place.

Let's move past the googly eye phase of the relationship to a seasoned relationship where communication and agreements seem to have trouble. The conversation starts the same. "Where do you want to eat?" The other person usually says, "I don't know. Where do you want to eat?" That is then followed by "I don't know. That's why I asked you." That is usually followed by, "Well, if you don't know and I don't know, I guess we are not eating." This is where the conversation gets sticky. The next response will either set off a communication bomb or an attempt to make peace and find out what you both will eat.

Some people will set off the bomb, saying something like, "Well, I guess we both won't eat, and we will starve because you are too incompetent to make a decision." WOW! Hold up! Is this the same person when we were dating that would eat anywhere and was open to communicating and agreeing on random things? Is this the same person with whom establishing an agreement was a breeze? Yes, this is the same person. The same person that just dropped that communication bomb in your lap. You have options. Remember, the goal is to come up with an agreement. You can often defuse the situation by suggesting somewhere you have eaten before. This will help the conversation move along in peace. At this point, it is not about the food but instead salvaging the relationship and ending on good terms. Making agreements is about building healthy relationships. Healthy relationships are based on the team's ability to communicate and support each other's decisions effectively.

Some of you may say the previous example of where to eat is not a significant example to share regarding agreements. The reason behind sharing that example is to show that everyone has had a conversation that involved agreements. The goal of sharing the example is to help others understand agreements are important no matter what level agreement is needed. Suppose you cannot agree with someone about where or what you are going to eat. You may struggle with other agreements such as where to invest your savings, which house to buy, or maybe even the kids' names. Taking all agreements seriously will help you achieve the goals you have set, whether about what to eat or which home to buy. Making agreements serves as the foundation for self-accountability. Here is how to identify the accords you will encounter as you increase your communication abilities.

Texting Shit

I received a request from someone on social media that I did not want to be friends with because of a conflict. As I thought about the person, their name stuck into my head. I then opened my phone to text my friend and ask him how to handle this request. Guess what? I ended up texting the person that sent me a request. Luckily, I was not talking bad about the person, but the person could see that I did not want to be their friend on social media. I stated, "Bro, "so and so" sent me a friend request, and I do not want them on my page." This was an embarrassing moment for me. I did my best to clean it up, but it was what it was. When texting, remember to stop, challenge, and choose. Stop what you are doing before you send the message. Challenge yourself. Do you need to send a text message or pick up the phone? Finally, choose to do the right thing. I did not use this process, and things did not go well.

Texting has allowed us to remove the human connection. This leaves a lot of room for miscommunication. Words that leave your mouth and enter others' ears may be forgotten, but written words never are. I know some people will only communicate in chats where the messages can be deleted. Stay away from those people. They do not trust themselves; therefore, you cannot trust them.

Writing words have a more significant impact mentally on the receiver because they will turn the words over and over and over until they come up with a conclusion about what you intended. I recommend only texting when the issue can be resolved in one or two exchanges. Anything requiring more than two texts needs to be talked about in person. Do not let the times we are in take away from using effective communication.

Exercise

Recall a time you sent a text message that you wish you did not send. Explain why you sent the message.

What was the message you sent?

_____

_____

_____

_____

_____

_____

_____

_____

_____

_____

Did you stop and think before you sent it, and if so or not what were you thoughts?

Did you challenge yourself on whether you should send it

or not, If not why not?

_____

_____

_____

_____

_____

_____

_____

_____

_____

_____

What would you do differently next time to communicate effectively?

_____

_____

_____

_____

_____

_____

_____

_____

_____

_____

Public Speaking (Talking Shit in Public)

Growing up, finding your voice was always a challenge in a house full of boys. Finding your voice was hard because everyone wanted to be different and identified as distinct. My grandmother often forced us, yes forced, us to speak in public at church. This was not my favorite thing to do. Standing in front of people and reciting a poem in church or in front of any group of people gave me anxiety. I dreaded Christmas and Easter every year because I would have to stand in front of people. I am an introvert. Doing this drove me crazy. I would practice in my room, memorizing the lines. I would go downstairs in front of my siblings and grandmother to recite the poem.

"Jesus died, Jesus lives..." and then my voice would crack. A knot would form in the back as if my throat like I was trying to have a baby out of it. It felt like I was trying to swallow the biggest pill a doctor could prescribe. The next thing I knew, my words started to sound shaky, and my palms were sweaty. My siblings began to laugh at me. I was holding up well until my grandmother

yelled, "ENUCIATE your words and start over!"

That did it. Down came the tears. The water fell from my

eyes like a category five hurricane. She immediately told me to go

back to my room to practice and get it right. After several

attempts and crying, I eventually recited the poem at home with

no problems. There was one problem left. I had to perform this

poem in front of an audience.

The day came, and my name was called to recite the

poem. Like clockwork, I started strong, and as I felt everyone

looking at me and the kids in the back laughed, I began to cry.

Welp, that happened year after year, and it was "my thing."

Everyone knew that Mike was going to cry at some point. After

many public speaking failures, I took a class on public speaking

while in college and learned a few things. The first thing I learned

was that my grandmother was teaching me to speak up. She

emphasized enunciation because she understood that it is vital,

especially when speaking to a group of people. My view changed on the importance of speaking up in public. I had to overcome my fears and deliver messages with confidence. Here are some tips for delivering a message in public.

- Identify what makes you fearful of speaking in public.

- Address your fears by talking about them to someone you trust.

- Realize that being nervous is normal.

- Practice your speech multiple times.

  - Practice in front of a mirror.

  - If you have kids, make them participate as your audience.

  - Present to someone who has no idea what you are talking about to ensure your information is comprehensive.

- Do not tell people you are nervous or if it is your first time.

- Leverage emotions by being sincere.

- Take control by owning the topic.

- Watch the crowd when you speak to gauge what is working and what is not working.

- Be authentic and let your personality come through.

- Use storytelling to reach people.

- Use Humor to break the room's silence and open people up for your message (when applicable).

- Minimize the words you have on your slide deck

  - The more words you have on the slides, the less focus you will have on you from the crowd.

- Don't read unless you must.

- Use cue cards to help prompt you, if needed.

- Give handouts when you are done explaining what you want people to know.

- Engage your audience.

  o Ask questions.

  o Take quick polls.

    ▪ Ask them to raise their hands if they agree or experienced something you are discussing.

  o Plant people in the audience that will respond to you to ensure you do not have any quiet spots.

- Watch your body language.

- Stick to your time limit.

- Do not rush or speak too fast.

- Know your audience.

  - Take time to understand the demographic of the people you are addressing.

  - Use their language.

- Send out a survey after your present.

- Test your equipment.

  - Do a dry run and confirm all cameras and mics work.

  - If you are showing a video, ensure it will show.

- Most Important- BRING THE ENERGY!

Scammers Talking Bullshit

If someone has ever scammed you, you know this is a feeling you do not want to experience again. Many people do not realize they are being scammed because they are usually in a happy state or desperate state of mind. Sometimes you may be simultaneously happy and desperate, which generally does not go over well.

Many people know that I love dogs and, unfortunately, was scammed by someone when I purchased a dog. I met a guy and knew him for about a year. The relationship was casual, and our shared interest was dogs. I was new to being a breeder, and he had been a breeder for over a decade. He noticed that I was happy about being a breeder, so he asked me if I wanted to co-own (share ownership of) a dog. The dog's price was high, and I could not afford it on my own, so I thought it was a great idea. He suggested that we would own the dog and keep the dog and breed it. I thought this was a fantastic deal. I could own a dog with someone and not have to take care of it but split the profits from the dog. I routinely checked in to see how the dog was doing and was always given an excuse for why I could not see her. There was no reason for me not to trust the person because he had never done anything to break my trust. However, I was concerned because I did not want the dog to be hurt or living in unacceptable conditions. After about seven months, someone advised me that they saw the dog on someone else's social media page. I immediately contacted my partner to find out what was going on. He stated the dog was living with his brother. I contacted his brother to see how she was doing. I learned the man owned the dog, and he was not my partner's brother. My partner had sold the dog behind my back for three times the amount we spent to purchase the dog. I was hurt and angry. I immediately reached out to my partner with the new information to find out what was going on. He finally admitted he had sold the dog behind my back. I immediately told him that we were no longer partners and that I did not want another dog. Nor did I want the money back. I was more concerned about his moral compass than getting another

dog or money.

What are some things you identified in my story that were

red flags?

_____

_____

_____

_____

_____

_____

_____

_____

_____

_____

Here are some things to look out for from scammers. They are ruthless people who only care about themselves. You are a pawn in their game. Remove them immediately from your circle and life.

How to identify Scammers

- They give you a nickname to make you feel special.

- They tell you that you have a great vision.

- They say all the right things.

- They may be overwhelming in communicating with you (You may feel like they are always checking on you).

- They always talk about the future to keep you focused on the end goal while doing shady stuff.

- Beware of odd phone numbers.

- There is usually no one that you can escalate concerns to.

- They have no website.

- Failure to provide professional references.

If the deal sounds too good to be true, it is probably a scam. Never become so desperate that you fall into a scam or become a scammer. You have worked too hard to get to where you are and earned all the money you have by doing the right thing. Do not risk it all for a quick dollar. Anything worth something in life is gained through hard work and dedication.

The Wrap Up

Speaking up is not easy, especially when you are put on the spot to do so. Speaking up can help change and save lives. Do not wait to be heard. The time is now. After reading this book, you have been empowered to control your tongue and your thoughts.

I look forward to you sharing your experiences about speaking up. Do not let people silence you when you know you are speaking up for all of the right reasons. Your voice is important for not only your future but those you come in contact with.